The Journey:
Bare Essence of Me

The Journey:
Bare Essence of Me

Naked in the Middle of the Street

Poems and Prose

Sander R. Holmes

Library of Congress Control Number:		2010914728
ISBN:	Hardcover	978-1-4535-6743-2
	Softcover	978-1-4535-5615-3
	Ebook	978-1-4535-5616-0

This book was printed in the United States of America.

To order additional copies of this book, contact:
Xlibris Corporation
1-888-795-4274
www.Xlibris.com Orders@Xlibris.com
84234

Contents

Chapter 11: When It's Said And Done

Dedication

Without certain individuals, this book of poems and prose would never have been possible. My husband is my inspiration, motivator, and sounding board. He provided many words of wisdom, and without him this book would not hold a special place in my heart. I thank my son, who has been my hope and a source of unconditional love, encouragement, and optimism. My brother, Kevin, who has been wonderful and supporting. My big sister Sandra, and my nephews have been a source of light in times of darkness and kept me pushing forward to the next day. Scott Jones encouraged me to write the words of my life experiences and thoughts down on paper, take one day at a time, and to find self love. A special thanks goes out to Pearl Mitch, who was instrumental as a contributing editor in *The Journey: Bare Essence of Me: Naked in the Middle of the Street*. All of these individuals are an intricate network of love and support, and I thank each and every one of them.

Foreword

Bare Essence of Me: Dear Diary

The hardest part about life is living it. You will be my sanctuary, my sounding board, and the truth of my life. You will hold the keys that are the essence of my soul. Only you will know the words that I write to be true. It will be only the truth, and you will see all of my faces, successes, and misdeeds.

It is you, diary, whom I will celebrate my triumphs with, as well as the feelings and woes that lie on my tear-soaked pillows. It is you who will be there when I cry, when I am in pain, when I am prosecuted, and when I am the prosecutor. You will be my conscience and the keeper of my soul.

You and I will take this journey together. You will be my best friend, my confidante, and my therapist. I will tell you who I was and the memories I have and the memories that will emerge as I travel along this road to find myself.

CHAPTER 1

A CHILD'S PAST LIFE

Everything Must Come Full Circle When Everything Is Known

I.

Everything comes full circle when the cycle is broken. The hate is in the marrow within his bones. He looks at me for the first time and his hate is known. I see it in his eyes. His large nostrils flare as he exhales.

What is this hate from this old black man that makes me feel uncomfortable as we stare into each other's eyes? Grandfather, Granddaddy—to me he's just a man I don't even know, but I can't take a stance. I visit him until it is known. Grandfather, Granddaddy—darker than my mother; I bear a resemblance to the woman we both used to know. That glare at me pulls me back and a tentative hug is something that I know, but I'm confused, and I think it is love.

Everything must come full circle when everything is known. The appearance of my face inside his home, a sharp tensing memory of his daughter named Rose. The one that wasn't fair-skinned, the one without green eyes, the one he called daughter that he wished he could deny.

I don't know all of their history, but it is deep within me, as deeply embedded as the hate in the marrow of his bones. Everything must come full circle when everything is known. History is everlasting, and I am his history and his legacy that he had to face. The face of my mother that he had many times attempted to break; never was described such a horrific beating she had to take. Eyes swollen shut and an unnatural deformity did he make upon her face. Everything must come full circle when the cycle breaks.

II.

The fear inside is here and keeps on coming. The anticipation of
the beating makes me want to vomit. Already chattering before
she gets home, "Someone hit me already," just to get it over.
Just a hot summer day and a square yellow fan stood in the
upstairs hall on the green carpet floor. A little toy car cradled
in my small, tender brown hand. The curiosity had gotten the
better of me; a simple-minded child's thought would surely
bring about my mother's fate.
I had to do it, just had to see what it would do. I stuck the little
red car in the yellow fan. It was our only source of cool air
that would move the flow of the night's air. One yellow blade
shattered into two and broke the flow, and everything would
come full circle and the punishment was a go.
Looking up at her with my pretty, dark brown eyes and
caramel-colored skin, my skinny awkward body felt each
striking blow. The folded brown extension cord seared into my
flesh, leaving lashes and welts all over my body, and the blood
would come from within. Sobbing uncontrollably but never
allowed to cry out loud, to do so would mean more lashes and
deeper-searing blows.
The ritualistic ceremony would continue the lesson of right
and wrong with hot water raining down crashing in the
ceramic tub. Submerged up to my waist, "get out of it," but I
couldn't take a stance.
As I bathed in the tub with the hot water burning my flesh,
when I got out there were almost no wounds left. Dried off
completely with my pubescent chest exposed and the white
towel draped around my waist, I received a hug. Tentatively I
hugged her, but she gave me a full embrace, whispered "I love
you," and dried the last tears from my face.

III.

The world makes me shudder and lashes out with punitive
blows. The anticipation over the consequences makes me
want to vomit. How do I get comfort to soothe my weary soul?
Nothing is right, I must have control. A razor blade, a box
cutter, or a knife, two vertical lines across my inner thigh. Two
lines horizontal to play tic-tac-toe. I'm in control, this is what

I know. As a child, that is what I had known, because that was what I had been shown; from Granddaddy to my mother and my mother to me. Everything was coming full circle, and I started to know.

I decide how deep and how long each cut should be. Showering in the hottest water and the would-be scars would go. I dry the last tears from my face and everything came full circle, and I understood as the cycle was broken. That wasn't love.

Grandfather, Granddaddy—everything I know, your legacy of hate had become buried in my bones, deep, so deep within my soul. Instinctively I knew this was wrong. I was my mother's child, and I felt I deserved each blow.

Never did my thoughts and actions that were linked to you ever repeat themselves nor go beyond me, but ended with me. Everything has come full circle, and the cycle of abuse had been broken, and a new legacy starts with me; my child will never know.

Lies Don't Matter

Apple, peaches, pumpkin pies—in your eyes I was nothing
more than a lie; the lie forbidden as was I. Untruths and
falsehoods, that wasn't I. I told you I mattered. I wasn't a lie.
Love and warmth, a simple word of kindness, this is what
I wanted; but it was always denied. No longer with just the
roll of your eyes, the shrug of your shoulders, the breath of
your cruel words, the sneer of your lips that showed cold
indifference control and flip my switch.
Apples, peaches, pumpkin pies—disappointed in the truths,
once we find out they were always lies, sweetness and naïveté
is no longer alive. All that existed in me were your lies. No
longer with a child's mind spoken with a child's word do I ask
for your approval and unequivocal praise.
No longer with a child's steps do I tiptoe around your rage. I'd
always be frightened that you will see me and curse me all the
same. No longer do I woe over the grief which caused me pain.
Emotionally and physically my soul you had once drained,
now I forgive you all the same.
Apples, peaches, pumpkin pies—we all grow up and somehow
survive. No longer viewing the world through a child's eyes, I
see the truth without the pain. I have accepted the truth and
relinquished the pain. I've grown to be wise; I see you for who
you are, the one who told me lies.
No longer do I need or want your conditional love. No longer do
I feel betrayed because you denied me love. Rejection is a part
of life. I've healed and wish you the same. To wallow in despair
and never move on or forgive, that would be the real shame.
Apples, peaches, pumpkin pies—from the beginning to the
end of life we are taught this childhood rhyme, not realizing
that in spite of lies, life can be as sweet as pie.

Ghetto Living

Living in the ghetto was predetermined by my birth. That's
the way it was. Learning how to conquer the ghetto turf
and staying alive despite my foretold demise. It was a state
of mind, a state of being; at times it was the sensuality and
sexuality that kept many of us entrapped in that state of being.
Not by choice, we had to learn to walk the ghetto walk to
keep others away, and talk the slang that kept others at bay.
We enforced this walk and talk even though we knew it might
allow death to take us away. Ghetto living—the same old shit
and struggles happened every day.
There were no delays; the successful completion of surviving
the day came down to knowing when to run and when to
throw fists just to last another day. But refusing to be trapped
in a generational pattern of poverty and self-hatred that came
from beatings is what determined me to keep my mind free.
Free from ghetto living—whatever did that mean? I pondered
at times as I looked around me. Where and how was my
freedom to be gained? Fences surrounded our place of living.
Were they there to keep others out, or were they designed to
keep us in?
Free . . . freedom from what became generational living; it
didn't have to be, but ghetto living simply wasn't for me. I
desired and fought; I made a choice to break free from what
was around me.
What I breathed, ate, and lived was only a part of me. Freedom
from ghetto living in the projects—it was a part of my identity,
but it wasn't my destiny.
But I learned from my existence there and from the challenges
I faced every day.
Inside my mind is where I dwelled every day to stay real, and to
keep pace with the raw hustle that came with each waking day.
That day a mother felt misery and pain as her child was slain.

What did I see? What did I know? This wasn't the life for me.
This wasn't how it was supposed to be. My blood, his blood,
came from within. The inescapable cries were subdued from
the shock that he had been shot. At the hands of his father
whose finger pulled the trigger . . .
Movement, scrambling, hollering, and cries; the blood from
my blood came from within. Strength from God is the only way
he escaped the wrath of ghetto living that should have done
him in. This is what I know; this is what I saw.
Ghetto living wasn't meant to be, at least not for me.
Freedom—this wasn't it. After that day, I learned not to let
liquor soak my lips. I understood not to embrace a weapon as
my force to handle my shit.
Being anxious and traumatized were a given, but they could
not rule me; I could not let them in. It would not endow me
with strength nor allow me to escape from the poverty that
kept me trapped, nor would it set me free.
My truest conviction was to survive with my mind intact that
would break me free from the unspoken generational pact,
which kept trying to draw me in. The trade of the day wasn't
going to be me. I would not find peace by letting some pimp
drug me and keep me. Even without drugs, I wouldn't be a
train ride or a disposable being.
I was a strong black woman, and the world was all for me; if I
just let it be, wanted it to be, it would be at my feet. My mind
was my passport, especially if I learned from everyone around
me. I'd set myself free. Ghetto living wasn't meant for me.

CHAPTER 2

Inside My Head

Listen To Me, Brothers and Sisters

I want to listen to you, brothers and sisters, and hear what you have to say. I want to listen, no matter our differences. I know we all feel pain. We all have personal demons that we hide in shame. Now listen to me, brothers and sisters of all colors, races, and creeds. Feel that pain and own the shame. To refuse to do so, you'll remain chained by the demons of your past and current life. You will never see change.

The fear of others knowing what we hide leads us all to tell lies. It keeps us from truly living and feeling in this life. That fear we share tells us to hide.

Those who we hide it from are hiding from us, but they just don't let us see or know. It's all a persona we each put forth to one another, all so we will glow. I feel you, brothers and sisters; I know the game and feel the pain.

The shame, hurt, and misdeeds we've done to others and others have done to us, it's all prescribed from the laws and morals we all have grown to know. Is it man's law or God's law, or does anyone know?

This is not to question the truth of any one god's existence, because we all have our own faith. Listen, brothers and sisters, don't let others dictate your fate to you based on their faith, their morals, and their laws; who's to say anyone is wrong.

Can you smell their fear? Because they can smell yours. Through our fear, they will control us all. This is not to say that there should not be laws or morals or that all is wrong, but question who spews out the laws and morals that make you hide in fear and continue to live in shame. Let them do whatever they feel as long as it does not belong to you, inhibit you, or stop you from seeing and believing in your own morals and faith.

I feel you, brothers and sisters. I share where you are coming from. We bleed the same color of blood and breathe the same air. Unless they walk on water, none of us should have anything to fear.

We must learn acceptance and be tolerant of each other. Spread your wings and let the shame go. Your god is my god and my god is yours; isn't it true that our gods want the same thing? Love and forgiveness. Even if you have no god, this life is yours to be free, and live life well and according to your own beliefs.

Prolonged Darkness

It's raining—lightning and thunder rule the shadowy skies, but
the true storm is inside of me. Trying to figure it out, what's it
all about?
Nothing but dark, murky, and bottomless seas lie within me.
No clear vision of the future. Aspirations left long ago.
Stillness is prolonged . . . maintaining the darkness in the day
as well as extended nights is hard.
As within me, the raining outside won't stop. Throw me a lifeline
and extract me from this bed of black rocks encasing me.
This is more than blue, this is something new.
Afraid to go to sleep and afraid to be awake, this is more than
blue, this is something new. It goes deeper than sadness, its
black walls surrounding me.
A living death, I have nothing left.
A lineage of secrecy and shame, I can't find a good reason why
this darkness wasn't proclaimed, so I could deal with it and
learn how to be free and live in the light.
The forbidden knowledge deepens the sadness.
Trying to figure it out, what's it all about?
The stigma of prolonged sadness continuously alters my life.
Perceived as a defect, my periods of blueness lessen the
credibility and validity of my self-worth.
My whole life and my existence are whittled down to this
profound sadness and others only want to define *me* as *it.*
But somehow, the rain always dissipates and the sun always
illuminates me; and the darkness of sadness goes away. Hope
is once again rejuvenated, and the black walls are no longer
surrounding me.

Whisper in My Ear

Whisper in my ear and tell me what I want to hear.
Tell me it is okay to know the truth of the world without the weight of its knowledge tearing me down.
Tell me lies to keep me blind from the atrocities of the ways of the world.
I am not yet ready to see the truth today.
I'm not strong enough now to keep my own power; no, not today.
But just whisper to me.
Whisper that today is okay to be vulnerable.
Whisper that when it seems as if the world is devouring me with lies, that
I have to get up and keep trying to make a change.
I have experienced and witnessed the pain, injustices, and shame brought to others by lies.
I have to believe that one person can make a change and a difference. Although I am possessed with worldly knowledge, I must keep hope inside and never let it die.
No rest, simply no rest.
It's time to get back to living, crafting, and dealing with this world; and co-exist with the truths of the worlds I wish were lies.
There is a way; there has to be a way to maintain my ethics and integrity every single day.
I must not stray and choose when to be right and when to be conveniently wrong.
Others are fine replacing their conscience and soul with money and lies, and assert their power over others.
They thrive on the misfortune of others and work hard to keep what they have to maintain the status quo.
It justifies the selling of souls and the lies that were told.

Their world is in order, and that's how they maintain it.
They really don't give a damn—ain't that a shame?
Whisper in my ear and tell me what I want to hear.
Tell me at the end of the day when I come out intact that I
faced the world with truth, without fear, and that I made a
difference in the world today.

CHAPTER 3

Stay Away

Nothing Convenient

From the beginning of my birth, you would always deny and
say, "She is not mine." Before I could understand the nature of
your worth, I was daddy's little girl and you were my world.
I would wait for you most of my life, even though I knew I
would be a conflict between you and wife. You should have
been man enough to stand up and claim what was yours.
But instead, you came into my life when I was twenty-four.
I had no real memories of you participating in my life, and I
saw you twice before my mother left this life.
This is when you left me to the world and my own demise. You
didn't care if I lived or died. That would be convenient for you so
you would no longer have to tell lies and hide me from your wife.
When I was growing up, there were no cards or words of
wisdom to guide me in this life. You didn't learn your lesson,
but went to another man's wife.

..

How could I be so stupid, still wanting to be daddy's little girl.
With open arms I accepted you. Never once did I ask for you
to earn the right to be within my life. It was absolution you
sought for all of the things you did not do right.
Unable to be around me and tell me about your life, you try
to buy my love with money, because your conscience was
strangling you because you didn't do right.
Not that I care now, but for years it baffled me how you could raise
another man and woman's child and not the child you gave life.
I made it alone and on my own. So don't claim my beauty and
intelligence as something of yours. Don't acknowledge me now,
because daddy's little girl is now a woman . . . and you're no
longer needed or convenient for me or relevant in my world.

Rage

Rage is an emotion that makes us scream.
Hot and acidic, it boils out of us and onto one another and
other things.
It is natural, but illogical.
We feel it.
Nothing we see or do makes sense when it comes.
Pure rage in its truest form is derived from the self-protection
that lashes out unexpectedly when situations overwhelm us,
and it is obviously wrong to our moral sense of being.
It is our most powerful emotion and yet the most destructive
of all feelings.
It is a part of us that usually goes unseen.
When unleashed, this force of nature scares both you and me.
It is a moment of temporary insanity.
Hush!
It must not be seen.
Others would call us a monster when our actions become
obscene.
But what provoked us for this force to be freed?
Whatever it was, it festered in us deep.
So deep and unresolved, it had to eventually be released.
But look around, it is always present and dressed in many
different forms that we've already seen.

Sometimes I'm a Dollar Bill

I am the cream . . . for cash rules everything around me, and I
am used to fulfill someone else's dream.
I am seen as the dollar bill for those with power to use at will.
My knowledge, creativity, and youth are used until my value
has decreased.
Out of circulation I have become.
New blood is infused into the system.
They get the new cream while I become nothing but a
lingering dream that builds the fortunes of millions, but
nothing left for me.
How do I get my dream without using someone else as cream?
I am the cream . . . for cash rules everything around me, and I
am used to fulfill someone else's dream.
They have dreams of living large, and I become the means.
Easy money they want, and I'm down and poor on my luck.
I want the dream, but I don't have the means.
Soaked in low self-esteem, no rope to climb out of the hole I'm in.
I become a part of someone else's dream.
My flesh is the dollar, and I am used.
I want the dream.
But I am the cream.

-

-

I sell myself for dollars to anyone and everyone who has the
cream, and I become a part of their dream. I give away the
dollar to the man that crudely rules everything around me.
Broken bones, swollen top lip cut with a slit, and a slight
stinging bottom lip.
I am the dollar bill that provides the dream.
When my value is decreased, I am the waste left behind after
all of them have gotten what they want and need from me.
How do I get my dream?
I am the cream . . . for cash rules everything around me.

Born in the ghetto, south side of town, projects lingering in my
future because education is substandard and I can barely read.
Trapped within these poverty-ridden buildings fenced in by
barbwire, and
I am by myself with nothing but broken dreams.
I don't accept it but that's the way it is.
Roaches crawling over me in the dark under my sheets.
I can't sleep at night.
Next door the man beats his wife.
Police don't care about the fight.
Because ain't nobody in the hood got the cream.
This undoubtedly tells me I am the cream to be used at the
discretion of others to build more dreams so that they may
reign over me.
How do I stop being the cream to build my dreams?
I am the cream . . . for cash rules everything around me.
I am the black oil deep beneath the earth.
I am worth billions in the world around me.
I am the catalyst of many fights.
They fly to get me.
Fight over me.
Die for me.
Those who own me rule those who don't have me.
When I'm removed from the earth and no longer fertile, I am
boarded up.
Never to flow again.
Cream is used, but never rules.
How do I get the dream without using someone else as the cream?
I just want a little taste of a partial dream.
Ain't nobody got a word for me on how to stop being the cream?
Claim it, take it, don't give into the fight of circumstance, just
do it right.
Get the dream and don't become the cream or use others to
acquire my dream.

Untapped

My rage is silent and seething inside.
Why don't I listen to the crackling fire that's roaring to come out?
An untapped source of fury,
I must allow it to flow.
The reasons it consumes me is unknown.
I am stealth within the world that surrounds me. Where is my voice? It is an untapped source muted by fears of what would happen if I dare to speak my words.
My emotions are kept sealed and need to be freed.
Until I am rage-free, there will be no sleep.
Sleepless . . . night after night, my mind won't stop racing. If it doesn't stop, I may not live another day. I must give voice to my pain.
Say it, whatever it is, unleash it, let it go far away from me.
It rides me in the night and sleep brings no peace; my demons evade my space.
The unknown source of sleepless nights continues to elude me; an untapped source of rage, I fear it will never move beyond me.
Shouting and screaming, cursing out loud, I scare others away who lie beside me. Violence is present. Nightly actions unknown, I must confront my unknown rage, while living in the moment of this very day.
My thoughts are controlling my mind and body. Memories are locked away to protect me, but now they are hurting me.
Today is the day that I must unlock them and face them without delay. Uncomfortable with the transition of change, I take each memory and strip away the pain.
I have the power.
I will not give credence to my demons that are rage, and I will not let the fear of them drive peace from my life.
I change my thoughts and my actions, for it allows me to fight.

I must speak my peace while standing tall; and even if I fall,
facing my fears will not destroy me, so I remain strong.
I have the power to change my life, give voice to my words
because my words have power to release my rage.
Then I'll have no more sleepless nights, and the unknown
source of rage will no longer be a vice within my life.

CHAPTER 4

That's Just The Way It Is

My Breaking Day

Awake and already angry today, I slide down to the end of my bed, and I cover my face with my hands. This day is already in a state of disarray. I shake off the grogginess and attempt to clear my head, collect my thoughts, and try to make it through the rest of the day.

I drive my child to school way across town. The hooker off Cusseta Road is on her way home. I stop for gas before I go to work. Seven thirty in the morning and these fools are already selling dope.

They call out to me; flirting with sassy, empty words. I know what they are about because I came from a similar block that shouted the same ole hype. They can't pop that smoke as if I'm blind.

I've already lived that lie. I nod to them and smile and wink my eye. I think to myself that things have got to get better today.

Construction on the road and it is blocking my way and delaying me, as if I need this shit today. I get to work and here we go. Jealousy is here to stay. These females think they're going to punk me today.

The instigator is inciting the stalker to try to play mind games with me, and my thoughts are already going astray. I want better judgment to lapse for one moment and then everything is on. If she steps to me wrong, it will surely shake my faith. I'll lose my job . . . just one slip, and her face will sting like never before.

I compose myself and move on.

I have to believe that things will get better today. I gotta stay right, because I'm one minute from breaking away.

If things don't get better, I just might break the law today.

My cell phone rings and it's a creditor trying to clamp down on me.

He said he'll take a check or credit card for my payment today. I tell him I don't have anything for him, so don't bother me today.

Oh, and he's brave—he insists he's gonna threaten me today.
Popping all that smoke and yielding those lies, this man does
not know I'm aware he's telling me lies; I'm ready to break if
he keeps pressing me. Listen, little punk, I politely say, it's not
going to be your way; give me your home number and address
and I'll get back to you later today.
My nephew dies, circumstances ain't right; police in my home
state seem to be on a permanent lunch break. The boss lady
wants me to lie, knowing very well I'll give a nickel to the state
and pay a dime for each signature I fake. I'm not harming a
child. Has she lost her mind?
And unless she will do my time and pay my fines, ain't no
way I'm going upstate, because what she's asking me to do is
simply and absolutely wrong.
A two-year-old child got syphilis and made the evening news.
My adjustable mortgage jumped up a point, foreclosure is
inevitable, ain't no food in the house. I'm sure I'm five seconds
from breaking away and defying the law today.
I just want to run away.
How am I going to make it through the rest of the day?
I close my bedroom door, turn off all my phones, I play Marvin
and Otis because they understand what I'm going through and
they sing the song of the life I lived today.
Sick and tired ain't got anything on me.
Then I digest my day and know that everyone is living through
their own breaking day. I lie in my bed just praying for all who
lived this day, because tomorrow God will make up for all of
these days.

Is It Okay?

Is it okay if I talk with you while I walk in this world, Lord?
I must ask your permission for I am the one who leaves you
and forgets that you never leave me and are forever present.
I must repent for not putting you first in my days that are light
and filled with joy.
I must ask for your forgiveness when I believe that I am
beyond the touch of harm and hurt and say I need no one.
Forgive me, Lord, when I stand in man's presence and bask in
his blessings and approval, although I am outside of your grace.
Save me, Lord, for I forget who you are while I stand and move
in this world that at times becomes a wasteland to me.
Deliver me from myself, Lord, when I pray for you to come my way
when things are wrong . . . that is when I remember your song.
From this day on I will live your way.
If it is okay, Lord, I would like to talk with you while I walk the
rest of the way throughout this world.

Something Got A Hold of Me

I search for the unknown that is very much unfamiliar to me.
I'm stuck in a place and don't know where to go.
What I want is within hands' reach.
There is something inside of me preventing me from grasping
what I want and need.
As perplexed as I am, I know it's not fear, but perhaps it is a
lack of desire that has trapped me here.
Where did my desire go? I keep questioning, how did I let it go?
How did I end up here in this empty place which feels like
there is nothing left inside of me?
I am weary and tired and used up and abused.
It was others that I allowed to take control of me and use me.
I have nothing left to give and still others continue to expect
me to fulfill their needs.
That is the answer to my question.
Focus on me and not on others' needs.
This is the time in my life to be selfish to fulfill my own desires
to prosper and live spiritually.
This is how to get my desire back, by letting go of those who
have a hold on me.

Suffer the World

Paralyzed by my own fear, I was consumed with racing
thoughts of what may happen. Tense and always unsure, I
trembled when faced with life's chores. I took a step into the
unknown, and it drew me back into my solitude of silence
where I was safe from the truth of the world.
My fortress, my mind; yes, my sanctuary was the safest place
for me.
And in there my emotions were not fused with the pain from
this world.
I lived in the world once and was young, brave, brazen, and
free. I decided that I would step forth and make changes in the
world with all due haste.
Armed only with compassion and love, it wasn't long before
the world decided to change me.
Still young but wiser, my visions and views became very much
skewed.
I would suffer this world and the world would suffer me.
I would not play by the corrupt rules offered to me.
I came out swinging, fighting, and screaming for my life, and
my very survival depended on me.
Yes, damn it, again I was going to change it, or it was going
take over me and leave nothing but a frail, skinny imitation
of what I used to be. The world kept fighting to wrongfully
change me.
Still on the wrong path, I came out again punching and kicking
in defiance and at odds of what the world expected from me,
immorality . . .
The world started to consume me.
I was no longer a creation of God, but I was a design of man's
flaws and laws.
Lies became truth, justice was not blind, and then I realized
that man was not kind.
I witnessed all I wanted to see and it shocked me.

The world was too hard for me.
I saw young men die and heard politicians tell lies. I heard babies cry from starvation. I smelled the bowels of hell coming from man's mouth. The sulfuric acid of man's philosophical base, I tasted and swallowed it and I was debased.
It burned my mouth and down through my throat, ripped out my heart, and corroded my soul. I then began to hate the world and the world around me began to hate me.
I lived with hate and anger too long, and rage became my force.
I grabbed a hold of the world again, but the world in turn grabbed a hold of me. The world would not let go, so I had to let it go. I retreated to safety before there was nowhere to go, nothing to see, and I hated being me.
Returning to my fortress of solitude, I licked my wounds in privacy and safety. My fears and tears became irrelevant, and my thoughts became focused.
Sturdy at my foundation, no matter what happened, the world would not shake me.
All that I endured, all that I suffered, this was God's plan so I would live in a world by God and not by man.
It is his strength that commands me and his love that wakes me. It is his will that drives me and his words that save me.
I will not suffer this world, but through God the world would suffer me.

The River

Life is a continuous white rapid river—flowing along, peaceful or extreme. It doesn't matter if we want to flow with the unpredictable crystal clear rapids. It is a force of nature. We will crash against the slippery wet sharp rocks, that grant no sanctuary to stop for thought.

Life continues to move on whether it is peaceful or extreme. At times the river of life will be serene and calm and show us more beauty than we've ever seen. There is a rare white flower that smells like honey; a mountain top so high it looks like it surpasses the sky. The air is so crisp and clean, so untainted by man that we can actually breathe. We may never want to leave, but life moves on whether it's peaceful or extreme.

There is no solid plan to defeat such a force of nature. The river will always run its natural course, and we are passengers journeying down the stream.

There are times when we tread in the water, never moving or going anywhere.

It doesn't matter whether we are stuck by choice or not, we wade there at least once in our lives despite the river being peaceful or extreme.

Tired of wading, sometimes it becomes hard to keep our head above the water.

Some of us surrender to the river's power. We simply give up and the reasons are never known.

Others drift along and all they get is what the river of life permits. Some of us fight against the current and try to swim upstream. Crashing waters bear down upon us and around us as we gasp and struggle for air to breathe.

The river continues whether it is peaceful or extreme.

We never learn that the journey downriver continues as we may fight all our lives trying to swim upstream. Hard as it may be, the fight continues with our act of defiance.

We never learn anything but heartaches and troubles that stretch into tomorrow.
It doesn't matter if the river is peaceful or extreme.
Throughout the journey down the river of life, most of us experience being lost. We may acquire peace or get stuck in one place that is not our dream.
At times we don't understand and cannot cope in the river's wrath, but the journey continues whether it is peaceful or extreme.
Many times we continue to fight and rebel, but eventually those of us who are lucky learn to navigate and maneuver down the river of life well.
Although our journey ends in the same place, it is how we journey and learn to navigate down the river that gives life meaning, because it is both peaceful and extreme.

This Is True

I am still youthful, but like many I feel as if I've lived two
lifetimes already and possess the wisdom of my elders.
There will never be a time when I can say I've seen it all.
But in my life I am certain of things to be true and never
changing.
There is always an uneasy peace in this world, but when
the time comes, there will be war. Our young will die, and
when the loser lies down, nothing will be learned. Yes,
peace without intentions is a lie, to buy time to do the will
of power-crazed men. I am certain that this truth is never
changing.
The experience of living in this world tells me right away
that justice often does not always prevail and laws are not
always legal. We live in a world where the absence of man's
conscience sows the seeds of mistrust and destruction.
Yes, I promise you that this is the truth, and it is never
yielding or changing.
Man will never coexist in harmony. Harm will be committed
against one another based on intolerance, indifference, and
religion. The possession and love of money breeds cruel and
ugly lies while crushing the truth.
Yes, I am sure that some truths will never see the brightness
of the day and never will change while I live each day.
A few leaders will emerge generation after generation. When
they speak the truth and seek unwanted change, like John F.
Kennedy or Martin Luther King, then someone decides that
the speaker of truth must surely die before others listen.
Unanswered questions of why and how the speaker of
truth died will circulate amongst us and throughout our
grandchildren's lives.
Yes, this is true and never changing.
I am young and I think at times my mind is playing games
on me with what I see and what I know and hear. I keep

saying I am not insane. The actions of others have shown me irrefutable proof that I am not insane, lost, or bewildered. I'm just living; trying to make sense of what is happening in this world of unchanging truths around me.

CHAPTER 5

INDEPENDENCE

Choice

Never knowing what life was supposed to be, my unrealistic
childhood dreams kept me safe from the real world insanity.
Day by day, alone and locked away within my mind, I forged
my script of my own reality. Peaceful and calm, courageous
and untainted, tranquil blue seas were given to me.
God granted and created a profoundly serene place for me.
I was spiritually new, uncorrupted, and unused; I stayed
disengaged from the world's insanity. Beautiful—how beautiful
it was to me. Time passed and my childhood had gone away.
No longer capable of whisking myself away into the fantasy
world where I felt safe and bathed in God's essence of love
and grace;
I was free from the world's harsh embrace.
After time passed, life took me into the world. Life shook me
and shaped me, and then reality laid out life's map. Life said,
"Here are my rules. Accept them or reject them, but they are
your choice, so you choose.
You can make money or take money without earning it. You
can be the victim or the victimizer. You can create or destroy.
You can give pain or take pain. You can kill or be killed. Only
living in reality can you exist in this world. You can forgive or
carry anger and hate in your heart and soul. You can be moral
or amoral; you figure out which way your soul goes.
Heed my words! Only in life can you exist by living in reality.
There's a price to be paid, and it depends on the life you
choose. When your body diminishes as time ravishes you,
you'll look back at that map of life, and you may regret the
path you've chose."
Life's voice shook the ground. Life's voice was speaking, and it
was God.
To be amoral is easy and effortless but true.
Heaven or hell will be decided by you.
To be moral is hard.

Sometimes it will bring infinite tears, and perhaps more each day.
You will gain and you will lose. The longer you live, you will
either run and hide or fight and survive. But it's all up to you,
you still have to choose.

He said, "I was the one who granted you life and allowed you
peace.

I allowed you to exist in your fantasies and now making you
live in reality.

The road you've traveled and the choices you made were
yours alone, and you've got no one else to entirely blame for
the choices you've made.

But throughout your journeys, I wanted to see if you would
come back to me even in the face of hardness, cruelty, and
pain. I wanted to know if you would still have the same love
for me and belief in me as in the beginning.

Although you have experienced life in this world, the choice
has always been yours to make."

I awoke and sat up in my bed as tears flowed from my eyes.
I thought to be amoral and to carry hate and anger was a
natural thing to do, but the opposite is a godly way.

I won't be used or a victim.

I will fight and survive in the face of what is wrong.

Getting to heaven was never an easy road to choose.

Because of the love of God and my love for him, I had already
chosen.

Go to Where You Belong

Go beyond where you are and to where you belong.
Don't be content to settle for someone else's dream.
Go to where you want to fulfill your life's hopes and ambitions.
Do not let fear steal your vision and lead you away from your desires.
What is it that we truly fear, that steals our desire to aspire?
Others' principles are imposed on us and we fear their wrath when they don't accept or approve of us.
We must strive to thrive and move beyond what others would have us be.
They cannot judge unless they are willing to be judged.
They are flawed like you and me.
Go to where you belong and venture unto your dream.
Find your true essence and love it endlessly.
Take a chance and follow the path of the unknown without fear and uncertainty.
Embrace life's charms and all of its harm. Feel it, live it, breathe it, and survive through it all, for it is the only way to go where you belong.
Standing still in time provides no growth; it leaves room for nothing but the same old unrequited hope. Inspire your hope, and push past your fears.
Go to where you belong, if you dare not follow your own vision of what your life should be, you will pay by living someone else's dream.
Fear not life; venture all parts and live a life of endless possibilities.
Step out of your world and into the real world of life filled with miraculous newfound hopes and dreams.

ME

Don't tell me who I am. I already know the truth of the good
and the bad of me. The right and wrong, the indifference, and
the ugly parts of me. I know the beauty that lies within me.
I don't need you to understand me. I make no excuses nor
indulge in any illusions about my existence.
I am me.
Don't categorize me or try to place me in a box to fit your
neat, stereotypical idea and disillusioned vision of me.
Who I am, you can never be. I am a pearl, an amethyst,
unique and precious. Acceptance of me brings beauty which
emanates from within me.
I owe no allegiance to man or woman. I am fierce, vocal, and
the truth is my whip when it flows from my soul eloquently
and smoothly, and intentionally departs from my lips.
The strength I hold comes from within, for I alone am the
keeper of my soul.
You see, I've been through the lessons and the fires of hell that
were forged for me.
I sinned, I lied, and I manipulated and cried. Perhaps I was a
slut, an angel, or not; you'll be surprised what you have to do
when you need to survive.
I was everything to everybody, a chameleon that fit everyone's
image and needs.
I was left to exist on my own with no one to hold, and no one
to touch me or tell me I was loved.
And thus, I still became fierce beyond impossible belief.
So don't tell me who I am or who I ought to be. I walked
through the fires of hell, so I make no excuses for being me.
I walked the roads of hell and became a woman and used what
I had.
Don't get me wrong, this world can be unrelenting,
unforgiving, and cruel.

I grew tired of dancing the dance of corruption and its amoral
tunes. I could not beat the world, but in my lessons, I became
of the world, learned the politics and social graces and
polished myself up for games that people play.
At times I was a beast and could and would never be
controlled.
When I was whipped and treated like sludge beneath others'
feet because they feared who I was and who I might someday
be, I survived it all and became me.
Like a beast not of this world with natural and logical instinct,
I gave back to them twofold what they gave me. I knocked
them down so they were beneath me, but chose not to crush
them; however, they would have crushed me.
A cruel unsettling truth about me is that I speak the truth.
Not interested in money and power, I tell the truth. I showed
compassion where none was shown to me. I know the good,
the bad, and the truth of me, and I still love me.

Independence

I want to be free from conventional and societal singular
beliefs that do not belong to me. I reject the image others
propose to cast over me.
I am free to live and love as I please. What I have within me is
too powerful; it won't keep. The bare essence of my nature is
beautiful and defiant, and I won't stop it until I am pleased.
If I choose to sin, my maker will be my judge.
If I want to be pious and feel that need, I will have that, for it's
a part of me.
So don't bother me with your small-minded thoughts and
partake in the notion of interfering with my nature that you
would forbid me to unleash.
It is my thoughts and my body that belong entirely and solely
to me and my maker.
If my body is not picture perfect and you object to its form, so
what—it is mine and not yours. I love my body and will not be
objectified to conform to your societal image of how it should
be perceived.
My body is of a goddess in any shape or form.
If my religion offends you, so let it be. How can your religion
or mine be wrong when they are both based on intangible
faith and belief? Let me worship as I please. In the end, we will
all find the truth about our beliefs.
If I choose to love another the world deems is not for me,
leave me be.
I do not care about their race, color, or spiritual beliefs. If we
choose to love and understand each other against all others'
worldly beliefs, look at what we would have accomplished in
spite of our differences, as we live and love in peace.
Do not look to me as the center of the world's woes because I
choose unconventionality.

Your life and the bare essence of your soul may be
unconventional to me.
So we should choose to live in harmony.
I am not your adjudicator, nor are you mine.
Absolution does not belong to us; therefore, let it be said that
we should not judge.

So, What About You?

I hate you, I love you, but it's all the same. You lie, you hurt me, and I always cry. You confuse me then use me, and so I grow tired. But I will take the blame, because I allowed these things.

You have schooled me on the darker side of life. Now that I am seasoned and placed you aside, I've changed the rules, and it is no longer all about you.

Mad, are we? Ain't that a damn shame.

And so now you want to curse me because things aren't your way?

You're bold and say I'm not a Christian, and as usual you continue to lay down blame. I wish you would take a note from my page and accept your own choices as you alone made. And unlike me you will never take the blame.

No more numerous sleepless nights wondering about what I did wrong.

I had to make a choice to be happy or not.

I had to save myself from people who continue to use, so that meant excluding you completely from my one God-given life.

I can breathe without you, I'm sorry to say. I feel myself coming into my own being. I have outgrown you where I now reside. When I cry now, it is because I feel alive. I wish you well in this life. It is time for us to part.

Good-bye. I have to live my life.

CHAPTER 6

Irony

Double-Edged Sword

It determines the survival of man and the demise and fall of us all.
Each man, woman, and child has it.
It is a double-edged sword.
It can bring happiness to our life or destroy us all.
If our desires are met, it is the catalyst of our inspiration that
raises us beyond our own expectations.
If our desires are left unfulfilled, we are crushed beyond belief.
It is the one word that has been buried within our being since
the beginning of time.
It is so powerful that not one of us can ever leave it behind.
It invades our dreams and controls our minds, intoxicating
once captured; if not, it consumes us and eludes us, and we
see nothing but useless dreams.
It is the conqueror of our emotions, the father of irrational
thoughts.
It is the puppet master of us all as we hang limp from its
strings.
It belongs to each of us, and yet we belong to it.
We are owned and enslaved by the very idea of it.
It is our survival and our demise.
It is hope, our hope.
It is what allows us to dream, thrive, and survive.

Oh, How Mighty We Are!

Oh, how mighty we are . . .
We are dignified in our own self-righteous anger.
We cast the first stone in our conviction to move others to do
right, live right, and to be like us.
Acting in conventionality, we fear those who are apart from us,
for they may intrigue us and we may lose our own way.
Oppress them, suppress them, and deny them any rights.
To have absolute acceptance of difference or indifference,
Armageddon will surely strike.
Oh, how mighty we are through fire and brimstone and will
cast the first stone.
Our intolerance is the phoenix which arises as law.
And now we have the right to fight and say that others are wrong.
To not punish them is simply wrong.
True to our values, killing is wrong, but we pass judgment with
our personal biases and thus we feel strong.
Based on our belief, we prosecute and render a verdict.
The sentence of death when completed is infinite, and there is
no turning back.
We go against our philosophical base.
So how can we be right when we ultimately show no faith?
What if we were wrong to take the life God gave?
What if it was me, and I didn't deserve that fate?
So I must tread lightly when sealing others' fates.
Oh, how omnipotent.
Oh, how benevolent.
We can be the ultimate plague of alpha and omega, of man
upon man.
Show us the light, dear Lord, I pray, for we have become
gluttons of power and have tried to take your place.
"Vengeance is mine," saith the Lord.
What will be your reciprocity to us when we leave this world?

The Loop

I don't know how it came to be, but I still dream of a world of
hope and peace.
There are no lies or alibis, just respect and truth for the entire
world to see.
If this could be would I be pleased?
What would have to be given for this to be?
Who would make the rules that will create world peace?
Would we all have to be and think identically?
Would we have freedom, or be blindly and willingly obedient?
Or would we all become the same?
Would we be content with this regimented life?
Or would we rebel and cause more strife?
Then would we return to my dream of a world of hope and
world peace?
It is circular thinking and just a redundant loop.
We wish for an idealistic world that can never be.
A dream of world peace will cost us our own individuality and
freedom, so we're right back to a world of no peace.

Too Much Time

Sometimes, we underestimate our own self-worth. Somehow
we get locked in and focused on what we are not and the
mistakes we naturally, innately, and ultimately make and will
continue to make. Too much time we spend on who we are not
and the mistakes we claim that we allow to consume us.
Too much time we spend believing that forgiveness is for
others, and happiness does not belong to us.
At times we allow the perception of others to define who we
are instead of allowing ourselves to be who we want to be. We
do not take forgiveness for ourselves and claim the happiness
we at times rightfully deserve.
Is it because we do not know our own self-worth?
Too much time do we spend accepting the negativity thrown
at us, which is an intentional act of admonishment to freely
give control over to those who wish to control us. But do not
believe the negativity.
Believe in your own self-worth.
Too much time do we spend conforming and surrendering to
others.
We must know our own self-worth by choosing to embrace
self-forgiveness and choosing happiness for ourselves.

CHAPTER 7

HUMANITY

Fear

You dealt me a losing hand, attempting to seal my fate
because of the color of my face. Before I came into this world
and breathed my first breath, you had already premeditated
my future and declared war on my life.
You took me from my motherland with no God-given rights.
In shackles and chains I swayed across oceans to see my
new land. You whipped and beat me so I would be willingly
obedient just as you'd like. My identity was erased, the native
tongue of my land I was forbidden to speak, my religion taken
from me and your religion given instead.
Throughout the generations, you tried to instill fear in me
through slavery, lynching, and rapes. By your own twisted
fate, the fear you tried to breed in me—yes, breed as if I was
livestock—ended up as your own fear.
As a little black girl who used butter and sometimes Crisco
to moisturize my face, I didn't fear you nor cared that you
existed in my space. I had no clue at that age what you were
trying to do.
You feared me and my potential of what I would be able to do
someday.
The possibility of failure or success devours you with fear.
A failure as a little black girl or a little black boy, you would
automatically label me as a hood or thug, a crack whore or
dealer, just a criminal with reasons to make your prisons bigger.
My success meant your failure and would stir your fear.
So the best-laid plans schemed against me were not enough to
steal from me my hopes and dreams or believe that you had
any love for me.
But I'm not fated by your hate, but I feel only sorrow because
you sealed your own fate in hate.
I have only peace and love for all no matter who you are, and
that will be something you can never take.

I Am the Protector of Freedom

I am the Protector of Freedom, and I give freedom. That is my motto as a soldier. I'll fight to my last breath. Integrity and pride is something a soldier can't buy. It is instilled within me from the first day of my life.

Absolute commitment is how I survive. I will show no less than candor when others' lives are on the line. Selflessly I put all my wants and needs aside, so you and I can have the right to speak in all nations without reservation.

Safety and security is what I provide. I am the ultimate warrior who protects our shores. I sail upon the stormy waves of endless seas, not worried at all because God and country will protect me. I fly amongst the clouds, vigilant and ready for those who decide they want to encroach upon our lands and destroy our rights. I will not allow anyone to take away our God-given rights.

I have traveled endless miles on foot and faced others on their own shores. I know that death may be around the corner, but I will not flee. I will face what lies before me, so others may breathe. Others may attack me, but they don't bother me. I am a Soldier, and I will fight for all of us to remain free.

So that you may have your freedom, worship in your own religion, live for your beliefs, speak without penalty, and have the right to thrive without costing you your life. I will always stand and watch over you day and night to protect our rights. I am a warrior, a protector of those in need. I am freedom. I am a United States soldier.

There are no others like me.

I Am

I am every man and every woman.
I am the dichotomy of all that exists in each of us.
I am an Angel of God and an Agent of Satan.
I am duplicitous in man's souls and the righteous moral
source of his heart and mind.
I am the reflection of the actions and deeds of every misdeed
shielded by greed.
I am forged from a world of iron and steel and cooled by the
rains of heaven so I can slice both ways.
I am good and bad, and there is no one to teach me what I
should be.
I am.
I exist.
I live.
I breathe.
I am the trouble that you see.
I am the fear you fear.
I am the one you hide from.
I am the side of you that you don't want to see.
I am left to my own demise to decide who I shall be.
I am.
I exist.
I live.
I breathe.
I kill.
I save.
I am greed.
I am the reflection that you see.
I am all religions, races, color, and creeds.
I am everything different that makes you indifferent.
I am whatever you believe me to be.
I am capable of man's hidden and secret dark atrocities.

I am the light that brings hope though no one wants to see this side of me.
I walk both sides of the line.
I am a shadow dancer, but you will never see me; you never wanted to see me.
I am the evil that others indeed do.
I am the softness of rays of lights of virtue from the parting clouds above.
I am the pure innocence that lost my way because no one showed me or told me I was loved or how to live right in the light.
I am the twisted thoughts of perversions that destroy morals and decay society.
I am.
I exist.
I live.
I breathe.
I kill.
I save.
I am greed.
I am the reflection that you don't want to see.
I am the last hope of man.
I was once you.
I am your child.
I am what you've always desired to be, if you only believe.
I am the future once you leave.

Lord, Show Me How

Lord, I am unworthy as your charge to be what you want me to be. Nor do I have the strength to march forward to do the task you lay before me.

I am but one in billions. For who shall take notice and listen to me when there are others stronger and better than me.

But I am your humble servant and grateful that you have chosen me. Now Lord, show me how to move forward with your creed that we all have forgotten or chosen to leave.

Lord, I will tread with vigilance when I speak your name and words. Mindful I must be with my actions and my deeds. Although I do not shout out loud that I am a Christian, I am in my heart, soul, and mind.

I show others who I am through my actions and my deeds. And so we shall begin.

Others stand before me in your namesake and testify that they are Christians, and yet their words and actions are that of a serpent.

When I am surrounded by those who speak your words without truth, my soul feels ill at ease and I become angry. But my faith is stronger, and I remember my task and promise to you that I will give my life so you and your word shall prevail beyond time.

Without you, Lord, we are testifying Christians with false words and misguided human beliefs.

Lord, show me how to do your will.

Show me forgiveness so that I know how to forgive.

Endow me with wisdom to embrace both lightness and darkness in man so we can care for others instead of showing indifference.

Lord, show me compassion so that I may give compassion to others who have not known it and known you.

Show me pure love so we can live in peace.

Provide me with tolerance so others may see and believe.
Use me, Lord.
I am your vessel to do your will. I will never forsake you. My
tasks are minor for what you have shown and given me.
I am your humble servant, Lord, and I shall always do your
will.

CHAPTER 8

We Can Do Better

Happiness

In the pursuit of happiness, we often go astray.
We travel down the road of conformity and eventually lose our way.
We cater to the whims of others just to be accepted and forgo
our own happiness for approval from some other soul.
Still we forget, we were never meant to be the same.
Our uniqueness and our flaws are what make us beautiful. We
do not need others' approval to make ourselves happy.
It is self-love and acceptance of ourselves that makes us
stronger, better, and happier even though we are outside of
conformity.

The Best That We Can Do

I.

My belly hurts, and I feel like I'm starvin'. Growling from the
hunger within my tummy, I wait for dinner. Small bits of food
are all we have, Momma say. No food stamps until the next
week and Momma's ashamed.

She's on the phone crying to her namesake that feeding five
babies is a hard fate. Is she gonna help Momma? I don't know.
I'm at the cracked door sittin' on the green carpet in the
hall with my knees pressed against my chest and my arms
wrapped tightly around my shins. My face is resting against
the top of my knees.

This ain't nothing new; I hear about our different daddies, who
aren't taking care of their responsibilities, so not one of them will
do. They make my momma cry, and I hate them. I pray like my
momma told me because sometimes I hate her too. I know it's
wrong. I'm hungry and my tummy is waiting for food. How come
we don't get the food stamps right now? My tummy is still empty.

It's cold outside. Good thing it's snow. My big brothers go
out there and shovel the snow away from people's houses
for money so they can walk without falling. Hard work for my
brothers. I see them in the cold, I know. Too many sidewalks in
the projects, and Momma still on the phone. She ain't sure she
want them out there in the cold. She don't want her babies out
there shoveling snow. I watch her all the time, and I know.

Too many things are running through her head.

She thinks she's hiding those tears from me, but I know, I
listen, I watch, I know.

She hate her life, maybe she hate me too.

She turns up the back of her right hand and wipes the tears of
fear from her eyes as she stands at the kitchen counter. She
tells me when I ask what is making her cry, she says,
"It's the onions, baby. They make everyone cry." But she ain't
chopping them and they ain't even skinned.

Later I hear my auntie in the kitchen, and I walk in. She looks down at me and roll her eyes.

She hate me and whispers she looks just like them people up the street, you know they ain't no good, think they better than us. Look at her, she looks just like them and she don't even need a hot straightening comb in her hair as dark as she is.

Momma says, it ain't her fault, leave her alone. Her daddy ain't any good, and she does look just like him. None of their daddies ain't no good.

I know what they're saying. They think I'm dumb. I don't talk much and get laughed at because I stutter. It's hard for me to read, but I won't let go. I keep reading and reading, I watch, I listen, I hear. I understand what they're saying, they just don't know. One day they'll know the strength that lies within me.

I know Momma loves me the best she can, the only way she can. She let me stay near her, but I catch that glance. It chills my soul each time it's thrown. I want to run and hide, but something is keeping me near. I know what that glance means. My daddy, the worst of all the daddies, wealthy according to our standard, is the cross I must bear.

I see more disturbing glances at me when my tummy is hungry and we ain't got no food to eat. All because my daddy ain't who he suppose to be or do what he's meant to do, take care of me.

I am the punishment my daddy gave her. I am a punishment to her, a reminder of what she lost and can never be regained. I heard it all you know.

II.

I know, Momma, that it wasn't the life you wanted it to be. I know I was the reminder of a regret for a promising future that you could never know. But I am here. Never really wanted, while you were alive and after your death. I watched you die, me alone. Your last words I can never let go. "Be respectful to your fathers. Show them that I raised you all better without them." As you fell from the light green loveseat onto the floor, I stood over you, never wanting you to go.

Many years later, I didn't remember that day, or many days after it. But when I did, it was a knife through my heart, a bullet to my brain, the pain of remembrance, I was never the same. Today I know of your pains and hardships. You did the best at that time with what you had. To be half of the woman you were, I would be glad. Many could not have endured the life that you lived. You were loved beyond infinite boundaries.

Be proud, Mother, I surpassed everyone's expectations of what they thought I could be. I learned from you as I look back with an experienced woman's eyes. For me, it is one child, one father; it had to be different.

The past cannot be changed. Our choices today shape our tomorrow. Life isn't fair for anyone at times. Our mistakes are our experiences, and hopefully we grow as our life continues. No regrets, Mother. It is our fallibility that allows us to forgive ourselves and others. Forgiveness allows us to love and be loved. This I know, Mother, because you never learned how to forgive yourself. I forgive both of us for the sins we both carried in our minds and hearts that did bare hate in the actions between us.

Throw It All Away!

I will leave it all behind. All the stress, worry, secrets, and trouble I have, I will throw it all away. For just one day, I will live just for today. I will experience the entire world as it is and smile.

When someone curses me, I will say, "God bless you." I will pray for them to feel the peace that I have. I will have thrown the malice and hurt away.

If I am harmed by anyone today, I will refuse to carry with me the pain, not even for a second of this day.

If bad luck should befall me several times this day, I will say it is okay. To think about it repeatedly will only change my day. I am of happiness and I will throw my misfortunes all away.

If my secrets should become whispers around me, I will remember that secrets are not for anyone to know. My secrets I will always hold. Although I should be frightened and inebriated with fear as the truth of them surround me I will not care, for it is I who must lie with them each night.

I will be happy as I throw their whispers around me far into the night.

For I have secrets, as you do. They are me and I am them, and I will lie with them and throw my fears away just for tonight.

Today and tonight will be my homage I pay to myself, because if for just one time in my life, I can say that this day I lived robustly.

I can boast of happiness and forgiveness and remember that one day in my life I threw all my problems and worries away.

CHAPTER 9

More In Life

An Ordinary Woman

An Ordinary Woman I can never be. I am not an Ordinary
Woman by any means.
I am not made of only hopes and dreams.
I am a queen to all nations and the mother of man.
I can change a man's heart with the slightest touch of my
hand.
I can change the course of history with a whisper in my lover's
ear.
I can give life and take life with the power I hold in the palm of
my hands.
No, I am no Ordinary Woman but a woman with means.
I can birth, rear, and nurture a child with unconditional love,
you see.
I am the one who sows the seeds and shapes the world
according to me and my child's deeds.
The fate of the world has always belonged to me.
I am no Ordinary Woman but a mother indeed.
This is the source of power that an extraordinary woman
wields as she needs.

Extraordinary Man

There is an extraordinary man that every man longs to be; that extraordinary man is my father and belongs to me. There is a light that shines from his innermost soul. It is his honesty and integrity that guides lost souls. He is the one that people come to so they can find their way home. His wisdom alone is worth more than any precious gems and stones.

He is a creator of life and a nurturer in strife. He is a warrior and a protector for those who can't fight. Every life he touches, touches another life; they carry love and spirituality which are pieces of his essence and truly God's blessings.

They become the strength of each link of the chain that is weak and went wrong. They are now sturdy in the face of adversity, and the chain is now strong. They have now become like my father and guide other lost souls home.

This is his legacy he shares in this life. Where others would crumble and be led astray, he stands still and does not waiver, and he cannot be moved away. His soul cannot be bought or sold like others who won't fight. He remains true to what God gave him, freedom to love others.

He stands on his convictions, which is part of God's own nature.

People want to know how it is possible for one to care so deeply, compassionately, and give unconditional love. It is no mystery; he is in God's favor and blessed by God's hand. He is not an ordinary man, nor exceptional, he is what God made him, an

Extraordinary Man.

Far Away

Far away in a distant land that I've never seen, the pounding
drums of Mother Africa call out to me.
I feel the rhythm of love as the riveting drums surge through
me like adrenaline.
I have no control over my body, and I am entranced as I move
to a tempo I have never known.
A dance of passion and fire controls my soul.
My true motherland, Africa, is buried deep inside of me. I let
go and move to the song that possesses me. I dance and I
dance without stopping, the steps of obsession have taken
hold of me.
It's freeing. I'm free.
The beauty of my body is so innately eloquent.
It moves as lyrical prose embedded harmoniously within me.
And I know right then that someone in Mother Africa is
dancing just like me.
We are connected body and soul.
Our heartbeats and movements are naturally in sync.
I am connected to the land that I have never seen.
I embrace my heritage that is a part of me.
It can never be taken or separated from me.

The Devil Sang Me a Love Song

I.

The Devil sang me a love song. He sings . . . a powerful
baritone voice reassures me it's okay. His song mystifies me.
Show no sorrow; put no emotions there inside for they will
make you weak when you are ready to take what you need.
Power . . . Control . . . Strength . . .
He sings this love song that makes perfect sense. I feel
confident, bold, and filled with power. His song feels right.
The pitch and tone of his voice is perfectly alluring. The words
entice me and excite me. I listen carefully and the expectation
of instant gratification is intoxicating when I'm told I can sin
without repercussions.
Money . . . Judgment . . . Lies . . . Disguise . . .
Everyday people do it and their desires come true. Why keep
and hold on to anger because they have sinned against you?
Why should you suffer at their hands and take the moral road?
Who will defend you when you are at your weakest, old, and
alone?
Who will take care of you as you travel down the desolate
road of life alone?
Weak . . . Vulnerable . . . Fear . . .
That is what is in store for you unless you listen to me sing of
the woes you should never have to know.
Just be with me and give me your mind, body, and soul.
I will be your deliverance, strength, if you love me and follow
what I have to teach.
Suffer not another day if you come under my wings.
Forsake . . . Eat . . . Forbidden fruit . . .

II.

Me . . . my life . . . my times . . . my legacy . . . for I know what
lies beneath the shadow under your wings. The song you sang
to others is the reason for any sufferings I and many have
been touched by.
You offer me nothing that I am unable to have doing the Lord's
will without damnation.
I have no apprehension of the road I travel. It is filled with
redemption, things you will never feel, and experience outside
of God's light.
Love . . . Saving . . . Forgiveness . . . Grace . . .
I am deaf and mute to the temptations of your song.

My Chocolate Adonis

My Chocolate Adonis, you're deep inside of me.
You are my love, my life, my soul, my religion foretold.
My Chocolate Adonis is what every black man is suppose to
be.
Strong, confident, ambitious, and cares for me.
You are perfection existing in reality.
My Chocolate Adonis, with us it was never about money,
fortune, or fame, the car you drove or other materialistic
things. It's always been our love and fulfilling our emotional,
physical, and spiritual needs. And you, my man, have always
been there for me. You give me everything I need.
My Chocolate Adonis, I tried to push you away because of my
own insecurities, but you stayed there persistent and showed
me what a man, father, husband, and lover is suppose to be.
You touch my soul; you fill my life with miracles and wonders
yet to unfold. You gave me the greatest privilege of all—a
child, our child, the of best life.
You stayed through the rough times and good times alike,
and raised our child who will carry the best of both our
qualities throughout his life. You raised our son and showed
him the path to be a man as you were taught to be. Only a
true man and father with a beautiful soul can shoulder that
responsibility.
My Chocolate Adonis, you know I can hold my own. You were
the only man who could reach me and touch my heart and
soul. I was a challenge for you, but like a true man will do, you
learned me and conquered me as no other man could do. It
was your touch; the kisses on my neck that sent chills riveting
through my spine. You were it for me, my equal, my challenge,
the only man for me.
I love you from deep within; you gave me your heart and soul.
I was blessed you let me in. You loved me in spite of my flaws
and gave my life sensibility so I would let you in. My Chocolate

Adonis, I miss you each day. I miss the feel of your dark
chocolate body pressed against mine, the texture of your hair,
your smile, and your embrace. I miss your touch, your walk,
and the way you caress my face.
Without you I am nothing but empty space.
My Chocolate Adonis, you have loved me well.
My life is fulfilled and our union surreal.
I complete you and you complete me.
My Chocolate Adonis, you are what a black man is to me.

My Gift from God

Blessings beyond blessings God has given me. At times I can't believe how happy I can be. Even in misery when life has ravaged every part of me, I hold and know that every day is not a happy day, but a good day because I am alive. God will lift me beyond any despair or disgrace I feel. I only have to hold.

When life strangles me and there is no air to breathe, I hold; because I know he will never forsake me. He removes the hand from my neck that would take my life. When life has whipped me and there is no clear way to get out from underneath the wrath of those that wish to punish me, God reaches from heaven and brings me into the light. I will always fortify my faith in God's will. And so I consistently hold.

When there is nowhere to go and I am isolated and alone, I hold. When my flesh bleeds and my time here in man's world makes me weary, I hold. He will blow whispers of healing words of his absolute power and holiness across my body, wounds, and scars; and breathe life into my soul. It is God's promise to me and, therefore, indubitably I hold.

I will never leave God, and he will never leave me. When I await his presence he always delivers.

God lays what I require at my feet. Blessings upon blessings are what God continues to give me.

The Brilliance of God's Beauty

Awed in your presence, I cradled the brilliance of God's beauty deep in my arms. I was scared that I was chosen to bring God's gift into the world. Trusted to care for you and totally in love with you and by you, I stared at you for any eternity and never wanted to let you go.

Overwhelmed, you were fragile and precious as I held you close to my breast. You were so real. Innocent and pure and filled with unconditional love, you freed me from my demons of the past and present. I knew I would always be loved.

At the moment when our eyes connected, it was already understood that I would love you unconditionally and guide you through your life. You were the one thing besides God that could bring change for the good within my world.

You were the defining moment that changed me. Who I was yesterday belonged in the past. Who I am now and will be, was determined by your birth. The things that you taught me from just being in my life, you are the brilliance of God's beauty that I would protect you with my life.

Loving you was the easiest thing I ever had to do. It was the most humbling, natural, and spiritual experience that God brought to me through you. Your presence, just being, and lying in my arms made me a better person and erased any turmoil that existed before the brilliance of God's beauty entered into my life.

CHAPTER 10

Light

Clean Slate

What would it be like if we were born with a clean slate? No preordained life or destiny already embroidered in slate. What if we were born without our forefather's hate or had to carry their past deeds that already sealed our fate? Could we walk through this world without others expecting us to be like those before us due to our race? What would it be like if we were born with a clean slate?

Why don't we know what a clean slate could bring? Blessed in God's eyes and made in his own shape, what if nobody knew we had been touched by his grace? What if it were of God's mind to test each man's faith, not knowing of our task how would we progress when faced to give another a clean slate?

Left to our own design, would we pass God's test of faith by embracing our brothers and sisters with actions and words filled with love instead of hate?

Or would the clean slate still be stained and denied by our forefather's hate?

Would we continue to speak empty words without wisdom and lie to God saying we erased our hate to stay in God's grace?

God has knowledge of what is in our hearts and minds. What if he deemed for us to switch places? Would we be kind? Would we then be so eager to seal another's fate and start from some other's stained slate?

I am you and you are me, and our fate between heaven and hell depends on eradicating our hate.

What would we do if we took each other's place?

Would we still use chains on each other; degrade, or spit on one another because we were born of a certain gender, color, or race, perhaps a different religion or faith and born in a particular place?

Would we pass God's test of tolerance and love, or would we
just speak empty words with no wisdom and lie to stay in
God's grace?
What if I was you and you were me? Would we be so eager to
switch places and live according to each other's rules?
What if our fate between heaven and hell depended on
whether we could eradicate our own hate?
Could we stand the test of time and change our thoughts,
actions, and minds?
Would love and tolerance be known instead of standing at
man's gate and guarding his hate?
What would we do if we took each others' place?

The Depth of My Hate

I should not confess that the depth of my hate was greater in
my youth. It was heavy and powerful; nurtured by simmering
coals ignited into fires in the days of my youth. It was married
to my soul. The hate was hidden behind kind words and false
intentions and superficial words of forgiveness. All was not
happiness and loveliness.
Thus, I had no soul and willing to admit that I privately
coveted hate.
I had become entangled and entrenched in self-hate, not
knowing it was my self-worth being destroyed because of my
own hate.
I grew beyond others' ideas of me and became more than they
wanted me to be and better than I thought I could ever be.
Self-love and forgiveness is stronger than the roots grown
from hate of one's past.
Letting go of the depth of my hate created love.

One True Thing Is Love

One true thing that will never change is falling in love. We
were born to love. Births will continue to bring life from love.
Life will continue until death claims us, but that love in us will
somehow still exist.

While we struggle between the time that we are born and the
time that God takes us home, we make choices that others have
made a thousand times before, which is to love and be loved.
We love in the purest form, never contemplating that it will
ever end. Our heart pounds away in the deepest part of our
soul and we surrender as we feel our lover's touch and crave
so much more.

We replay over and over the moisture from a sensuous kiss
that lingers far beyond our expectations. We're free in love
and of love, no boundaries or barriers. We're swept away in
this uncontrollable helpless feeling.

We're feeling it and holding on to it for dear life, because we
never want it to end.

But some things will never change.

Love begins and sometimes it ends.

Everything that shined, everything about love that nurtured
what we felt is no more. Our chest becomes so tight, and our
throat is constricted that we cannot swallow and breathe the
very air we need to sustain our life.

It's unexplainable and inexplicable what we gave and received
from love.

When it's gone, we are still in need of that craving which
brought us and showed us the truest sense of our self.

We find that we have the capacity to be and have a great love.
We make our mistakes in love and sometimes we grow from it.
Other times we let our love that ended break us and remain
stagnant and confused, vowing to never love again.

Why do we wallow in so much despair and not recapture the essences of the experience of love? We have to go forward and learn to love again.

What we were at that time we can never be again, but we can take the best of what we had to become a better lover for a new beginning of possibilities and ideas of what we believe love can be.

We will find a new type of love to satisfy our needs. A special love to embrace, because one thing is true: being and falling in love will never change. Without love, emptiness is all we have.

Shine Bright

This is not your time to hide, but your time to shine and take
flight into the world. Under my wings you shall not remain,
that is where you shall not grow.
Therefore, like others I must face my fears and let you go.
There are no words that I can speak to ease your mind from
the fear you have to live through.
What you have in this life will be determined by quenching
your fears and by seeking out your passions and desires.
Fear is only a perception that you must fight through in order
to know the beauty of the unknown that will unfold peacefully
before your eyes.
Fear will be your consummate companion and your failure if
you allow it to consume you.
To gain your wants and desires, your fear must pass through
you so you may taste the sweetness of this life.

Silver Fox

Silver all over, the color of our hair, we've entered the age of wisdom.
We should be revered.
We may move a little slower, but we are truly blessed.
Outsiders look at us, hand in hand and some feel pity for us because we have grown old.
Others turn away from us refusing to see who we are.
If they are lucky, they may be destined to be people like us.
We showed strength and courage when we climbed many mountains and triumphed through woes and heartbreaks throughout our years, and yet we survived to grow very old together.
They don't know that our lives were perfect with each other.
We grew together and never apart.
We are alive and living and still loving one another because our lives are still as beautiful as when we began our love, and now we start over again and together in our silver fox years.

CHAPTER 11

When It's Said And Done

Angels Can Say Prayers Too

Mother, as I received your prayers last night in the heavens
up above, I wondered if you knew that angels can say prayers
too. I pray for you throughout the day, because I know that
you are in dismay. And although my days are no longer spent
with you, know that I will always say these prayers for you.
In the morning when you rise and you are unwilling to face
another day without me, be still. God will soothe and heal
your soul. He will give you the will and strength to go on. And
so you do, this is my prayer for you.
As the evening befalls you and a gentle breeze lightly caresses
your face, know that it is just me touching you with God's
grace. And through it all because you kept your faith, you are
now held in God's pure and loving embrace.
Night has suddenly come and slumber has eluded you. You
cry for me. God knew you never wanted to say good-bye to
me. He has heard your cries and placed me, his angel, at your
side. As you fall asleep and I sway you in my arms, your tears
and woes will no longer weigh your soul.
Each day that you greet a new sunrise, please know that
your love given freely to me, allowed me to become the man
God wanted me to be. I was a man of strength and deep
compassion that lived his life with complete and pure passion.
And so unto you, as a son can only do, I now return this love
back to you.
I love you.
And although God has called me home to fulfill a greater plan,
a plan that he alone understands. Just knowing how much I
cherished you was God's way of healing you. So now you have
hope, and life will be renewed because angels' prayers are
answered too.

I Know the Truth of It

Each morning the chirping songs of the birds are heard
outside of my window as they fly from tree limb to tree limb. I
know the truth of the songs of life they sing. I am alive. It is a
new day. As the sun blossoms over a new horizon into a bright
day, the promise of hope starts my inevitable day.

I know the truth of a new day.

Life is built by moments.

Yesterday cannot be redeemed.

Time pushes forward and will never stop. The transgressions
and wrongs cannot be erased. I know the truth of that.

We only have to believe and know that what cannot be erased
can only be cleansed by prayer and forgiveness.

The sun will rise another day, and if we are lucky, we will be
blessed to live our lives another day.

Forward and onward. We must leave yesterday's regrets
behind us. They serve no purpose on this day. To linger in the
past, all that I am will diminish, and hope of what can be will
simply float away. I know the truth of it.

Live for today and tomorrow.

For I am fallible and imperfect. Acceptance of my duality of
good and bad is the breath of my life.

So I accept it, and I breathe.

I see and appreciate what is within my sight. Here and now,
the hope for tomorrow. Live for what can be and not for
what was.

In My Own Defense

I.

Today I met my maker and fell upon my knees. I confessed to
him, "Lord, I know you're not pleased." The sins I committed,
the lies I told, the evil thoughts and actions—God, you know
my soul.

But let me say in my own defense, I was lost in this world with
an empty soul. I felt and knew fear. I denied responsibility for
the things that I did. I blamed others for my sins and put forth
an image of purity so no one could see me from within.

I enjoyed the sufferings from the pain I caused with righteous
indignation; I reveled in satisfaction in my defeat of others.

I manipulated anything and everything and justified it as a
human thing, when wronged; doesn't every man or women do
the same?

I played the game in life and perhaps I played it too well, even
though I knew it could buy me a one-way ticket straight to
hell.

As I grew older and time passed by, my soul continued to feel
empty and so I told more lies. But then my body became old
and faced with mortality and loved ones continued to die; I
began to fear death because judgment day was nearby.

II.

An epiphany came to me one day, but I know not the time of
day.

A natural progression of the truth of my life was clear to see.
I spent my days in hurt and anger forged into rage. I reacted
without thought or reason, lashed out at those who had
harmed me. I was jaded and could not see, and I accepted all
actions of others who were malicious, selfish, and cruel to me
to define who I would be.

Their actions became the fate of others who had done nothing
to me. It was this anger and rage I embraced and not peace.

Embedded deep inside, my hate of the world consumed me in
ways I couldn't explain. My body and mind began to fail me.
Helpless and unhappy and no one to turn to, I created my fate
of loneliness that dwelled and kept me from the real world
which was too much pain to keep.
I had to recapture the real me; reconnect with who I was
before I allowed the world to take me. I testified to God and
made my peace, as God brought me out of darkness and the
real me emerged. I embraced who I was and who I would
never be. The dreams of unrealistic hopes and tangible things
I didn't need. My honesty relieved my burdens of hiding from
all things. The caring and compassion for others God gave
back to me.
God has forgiven and loved me, and so I made peace with
myself living in this world. God's word is never breached. I
repented and he gave me peace and showed me his greatness
where I didn't need to ever say again, "In my own defense."

Making My Peace

When I make my peace with this world and life is said and done, my last breaths will be as precious as pearls. I will let the last waters of life run down my face because my spirit will be free as I depart this world.

I know that physical death is absolute. There will be no last minute reprieve or bargains to strike to save my life. My judgment will be swift and there will be no excuses justifying the way I lived. But that is tomorrow, for this very moment I live.

Thinking of this is how I take stock of my life and live my life. I live hard and love deep. I run across the lands and seas barefoot and wild and free.

Laughing as I soar in the skies above, it is the pleasure of life and adventure that I adore. I feel the wind's fingers strum through my hair. It is the blood that rushes through my veins that tells me life is real.

This is my world; I take it and I am free. Others who judge me, I leave them be.

Those who try to steal my joy, I think how sad they must be. I wish them all the happiness that life can give for them to keep. When sins confront me and are within hands' reach, I ask how much my soul is worth—a nickel, a dime, a penny, or a lie? No. I think before I indulge, before I sell my soul; I shall remain free.

I promised myself that I would not waste my life. Entering into others' fallacies is not for me. Each breath I take is filled with passion. The words I speak must count; it is my conviction that I feel in this life. I build each part of my world based on love and peace. So when I make peace I will still be free.

Where You Will Find Me

My last thoughts are racing thoughts of you. They are not of tangible things and unfulfilled desires of this world. Think of me by the words, deeds, and experiences I have shared with you about my life. This is where you will find me deep inside your mind.

The memories of the moments of a child looking from an upstairs window, I have seen the autumn colors of trees of auburn and red and yellow mixed with green. They were enraptured by a clear blue sky that gave me such clarity.

In the hills of Pennsylvania, I breathed the fresh air. I drank from a fresh stream of water without any fears. In these times, I memorized the image of beauty I would never experience again. I shared the memory of being there with you so you would know of another time and place where I found beauty and never knew despair. Keep that purity of no fear or despair as part of you.

Remember my favorite time of day when heaven existed on earth. The morning is always a new chance to begin again. The chirping of the birds flutter through the air. I cannot see them, but their songs soothed my soul.

Dew dropped from the green blades of grass and nurtured the ground of our land. Our bodies melted together. I was where I belonged in your arms with my head against your chest, listening to your heartbeat that filled me with peace. This is where I wanted to stay during the entire day. Remember where I laid, and the warmth of my voluptuous body and the smell of my hair. For in your mind, this is where I shall always remain.

Remember our youth when we had no cares. Remember how we ran in the rain and sang love songs to each other on bended knees without feeling silly because we believed. We believed in all our hopes and dreams. Our impetuous

youthfulness allowed us to share in the moment without forethought of failure, without thought of a skewed vision of what tomorrow would bring. Remember my laughter and fearlessness. In your hopes is where I'll be.
Never shall I be far from you as long as you remember me.

Edwards Brothers,Inc!
Thorofare, NJ 08086
04 March, 2011
BA2011063